SRA Reading Mastery

Signature Edition

Curriculum-Based Assessment and Fluency Teacher Handbook
Grade 1

Siegfried Engelmann
Elaine C. Bruner

McGraw Hill SRA

Columbus, OH

Table of Contents

Reading Mastery Alphabet **1**

Introduction **2**

The Placement Test **4**

Placement Test Scoring Sheet **5**

Fluency: Rate/Accuracy Checkouts **7**

Lesson 5 . . . . **9**
Lesson 10 . . . . **10**
Lesson 15 . . . . **11**
Lesson 20 . . . . **12**
Lesson 25 . . . . **13**
Lesson 30 . . . . **14**
Lesson 35 . . . . **16**
Lesson 40 . . . . **18**
Lesson 45 . . . . **20**
Lesson 50 . . . . **22**
Lesson 55 . . . . **24**
Lesson 60 . . . . **26**
Lesson 65 . . . . **28**
Lesson 70 . . . . **30**
Lesson 75 . . . . **32**
Lesson 80 . . . . **33**
Lesson 85 . . . . **35**
Lesson 90 . . . . **36**
Lesson 95 . . . . **37**
Lesson 100 . . . . **38**
Lesson 105 . . . . **39**
Lesson 110 . . . . **40**
Lesson 115 . . . . **41**
Lesson 120 . . . . **42**
Lesson 125 . . . . **43**
Lesson 130 . . . . **44**
Lesson 135 . . . . **45**
Lesson 140 . . . . **46**
Lesson 145 . . . . **47**
Lesson 150 . . . . **48**

Lesson 155 . . . . **49**
Lesson 160 . . . . **50**

Curriculum Based Assessments

Lesson 20 . . . . **52**
Lesson 40 . . . . **56**
Lesson 60 . . . . **59**
Lesson 80 . . . . **62**
Lesson 100 . . . . **65**
Lesson 120 . . . . **69**
Lesson 140 . . . . **72**
Lesson 160 . . . . **75**

Appendix **78**

Individual Fluency Checkout Chart **79**
Fluency: Rate/Accuracy Checkout
    Recording Form **80**
Interpreting the Test Results **82**
Individual Skills Profile Chart **83**
The Group Point Chart **85**

Additional Resources **87**

Individual Fluency: Rate/Accuracy
    Checkout Recording Form **89**
Reading Mastery Accelerated
    Instruction Schedule **91**

Reading Mastery Alphabet

Use this alphabet chart for determining whether a student is able to produce the sound associated with each symbol in the Reading Mastery alphabet.

Symbol	Pronounced	As in	Voiced or Unvoiced*
a	aaa	a̲nd	v
m	mmm	ra̲m̲	v
s	sss	bus̲	uv
ē	ēēē	e̲at	v
r	rrr	ba̲r̲	v
d	d	ma̲d̲	v
f	fff	stu̲ff̲	uv
i	iii	i̲f	v
th	thththth	th̲is and ba̲the̲ (not thing)	v
t	t	ca̲t̲	uv
n	nnn	pa̲n̲	v
c	c	ta̲c̲k	uv
o	ooo	o̲x	v
ā	āāā	a̲te	v
h	h	h̲at	uv
u	uuu	u̲nder	v
g	g	ta̲g̲	v
l	lll	pa̲l̲	v
w	www	wo̲w̲	v
sh	shshsh	wi̲sh̲	uv

Symbol	Pronounced	As in	Voiced or Unvoiced*
Ī	(the word I)		v
k	k	ta̲ck̲	uv
ō	ōōō	o̲ver	v
v	vvv	lo̲v̲e	v
p	p	sa̲p̲	uv
ch	ch	tou̲ch̲	uv
e	eee	e̲nd	v
b	b	gra̲b̲	v
ing	iiing	si̲ng̲	v
Ī	īīī	I̲ce	v
y	yyy	y̲ard	v
er	urr	broth̲er̲	v
x	ksss	o̲x̲	uv
oo	oooo	m̲oo̲n (not look)	v
J	j	jud̲g̲e	v
ȳ	īīī	m̲y̲	v
wh	www or wh	wh̲y̲	v or uv
qu	kwww (or koo)	qu̲ick	v
z	zzz	bu̲zz̲	v
ū	ūūū	u̲se	v

*Voiced sounds are sounds you make by vibrating your vocal chords. You do not use your vocal chords for unvoiced sounds—you use air only. To feel the difference between voiced and unvoiced sounds, hold your throat lightly and say the sound *vvv*. You will feel your vocal chords vibrating. Then, without pausing, change the sound to *fff*. The vibrations will stop. The only difference between the sounds is that the *vvv* is voiced and the *fff* is not.

Sound Combinations, Digraphs, and Diphthongs

al (a̲l̲so)	er	sh
ar (a̲r̲m)	ing	th
ch	oo	wh
ea (m̲ea̲t)	ou (o̲u̲t)	
ee (n̲ee̲d)	qu	

Introduction

This curriculum-based assessment and fluency system for *Reading Mastery Signature Edition,* Grade 1 is a complete system for monitoring student performance in the program. By using the curriculum-based assessment and fluency system, you can

- ensure that students are properly placed in the program
- measure student achievement within the program
- identify the skills that students have mastered
- maintain individual and group records
- administer remedial exercises

The materials for the curriculum-based assessment and fluency system consist of this Handbook and a separate Student Book for each student. The Student Book contains a placement test, a series of assessments, and passages for fluency checkouts. The Handbook contains instructions for administering the assessments and fluency checkouts, remedial exercises for each assessment, Individual Skills Profile Chart, Group Summary Chart, and an Individual Fluency: Rate/Accuracy Chart.

The Assessments

Two kinds of assessments are used in the curriculum-based assessment and fluency system: the placement test and the assessments. The Placement Test is administered individually to all students at the beginning of the school year. The results indicate whether a student should begin *Reading Mastery,* Grade 1 with Lesson 1 or Lesson 11. The results are helpful for determining how to group students for reading. Directions for administering the Placement Test appear on page 2. A reproducible form is included in this manual on page 5 for recording student performance.

For further information about first-of-the-year placement testing, refer to the *Reading Mastery Series Guide,* which includes Placement Tests for all levels of the program.

The assessments are criterion referenced, which means they assess each student's achievement within the program. Each assessment item measures student mastery of a specific skill or concept taught in Reading Mastery, Grade 1. There are eight assessments, one for every twenty lessons. The assessments measure student mastery of specific skills taught in *Reading Mastery,* Grade 1.

Decoding skills are measured by the individual fluency: rate/accuracy checkouts. These checkouts assess students' decoding skills at various points throughout *Reading Mastery,* Grade 1. There are 32 checkouts, which correspond to every fifth lesson starting with Lesson 5. The lesson number appears at the bottom of each checkout. To pass a fluency checkout, the student must read a selection within a specified period of time and error limit. The length of the selections and the time vary from checkout to checkout. The fluency checkout passages, along with further instructions, begin on page 7.

The Remedial Exercises

In order to pass each curriculum-based assessment, a student must answer at least 80% of the items correctly. The remedial exercises are designed to help students scoring less than 80% on the curriculum-based assessments. Each assessment has its own set of remedial exercises. The exercises provide a general review of the assessed skills, using examples different from those on the assessment. There is a specific remedial exercise for every assessed skill.

Instructions for administering the remedial exercises are contained in this Handbook. For some remedial exercises, the teacher is instructed to present exercises from the Presentation Books. For other remedial exercises, the teacher presents exercises written specifically for this Handbook. The presentation techniques are the same for both types of exercises.

Script Conventions

The following script conventions are used in this Handbook:

- This typeface indicates what you say.
- **This typeface indicates words that you emphasize.**
- (This typeface indicates what you do.)
- *This typeface indicates the students' responses.*

The Charts

Three charts are used in the curriculum-based assessment and fluency system: the **Individual Skills Profile Chart, the Individual Fluency: Rate/Accuracy Chart,** and the **Group Point Chart.**

The Individual Skills Profile Chart, for curriculum-based assessments of lessons 20-160, appears on page 83 of this Handbook. The chart lists specific skills taught in *Reading Mastery* and indicates which curriculum-based assessment items measure student mastery of those skills. When the chart is completed, it shows how well a student has mastered those *Reading Mastery* skills.

The Group Point Chart summarizes the group's scores on the mastery tests and fluency checkouts. It appears on page 85 of this Handbook. The chart provides you with an objective measure of the group's progress and can be used to evaluate the group's overall performance.

The Individual Fluency: Rate/Accuracy Checkout Recording Form summarizes the group's scores on the mastery tests and fluency checkouts. It appears on page 80 of this Handbook. Instructions for administering the mastery tests and fluency checkouts appear in the Presentation Books for *Reading Mastery,* Grade 1.

Assessments

The Placement Test

For the *Reading Mastery* Placement Test, each student reads a story aloud, as you count the student's decoding errors.

You will need to make one copy of the story on page 4. You should administer the test in a place that is somewhat removed from other students, so that they will not overhear the testing.

Use the following procedures to administer the Placement Test.
1. (Give the student a copy of the story.)
2. (Point to the passage and say:) I want you to read this story out loud. Take your time. Start with the title and read the story as well as you can.
3. (Time the student and make one tally mark for each error. Use the following guidelines when tallying errors.
- (If the student misreads a word, tell the student the word and mark one error.)
- (If the student sounds out a word incorrectly and then correctly, mark one error.)
- (If the student sounds out a word instead of reading it normally, mark one error. Note: Correct the student the first time the student sounds out a word. Ask the student, What word is that? If the student reads the word correctly, do not mark and error. Do not correct the student on any subsequent sounding-outs.)
- (If the student does not identify a word within four seconds, tell the student the word and mark one error.)
- (If the student skips a word, point to the word. If the student does not read the word correctly, mark one error.)
- (If the student skips a line, point to the line. If the student does not read the line correctly, mark one error.)
4. (After two and a half minutes, stop the student. Count every word not read as an error. For example, if the student is eight words from the end of the passage at the end of the time limit, count eight errors.)
5. (Total the student's errors.)

Placement Guidelines

(Place your students as follows:)
- (Students who made 0 to 3 errors are should be placed in Lesson 11 of *Reading Mastery,* Grade 1.)
- (Students who made 4 to 8 errors should be placed in Lesson 1 of *Reading Mastery,* Grade 1.)
- (Students who make more than 8 errors should be placed in *Reading Mastery,* Grade K. To determine an appropriate placement for these students, give them the individual fluency: rate/accuracy checkouts from *Reading Mastery,* Grade K. Start with the check out for Lesson 140. If the student passes this fluency checkout, place the student in Lesson 141. If the student does not pass this fluency checkout, present the fluency checkout for Lesson 130. Continue working backward until the student passes a fluency checkout. Place the student in the lesson that follows the fluency checkout lesson.)

the cow on the rōad

lots of men went down the rōad in a little car.

a cow was sitting on the rōad. sō the men ran to the cow. "wē will lift this cow," they said.

but the men did not lift the cow. "this cow is sō fat wē can not lift it."

the cow said, "I am not sō fat. I can lift mē." then the cow got in the car.

the men said, "now wē can not get in the car." sō the men sat on the rōad and the cow went hōme in the car.

the end

Placement Test Scoring Sheet

Student Name	No. of Errors	Comments

Fluency: Rate/Accuracy Checkouts

Fluency: Rate/Accuracy Checkouts

Fluency: Rate/Accuracy Checkouts can be used for placing mid-year students. For example, if you have two groups in your class, one group just completing Lesson 55 and the second just completing Lesson 75, begin by administering the fluency checkout from Lesson 55. If the student passes that, administer the fluency checkout from Lesson 75. If the student fails the Lesson 75 fluency checkout, place the student in the Lesson 55 group; if the student passes the lesson 75 fluency checkout, place the student in the other group.

Procedure for Administering Fluency: Rate/Accuracy Checkouts

Use the following procedure to administer the fluency checkouts.
* Identify a part of the room or another setting where a student can read to you individually.
* Sit next to the student.
* Tell the student when to begin reading.
* Start the timer and note the time.
* Observe the text that the student reads.
* Make a tally mark on the recording form for each error.
* Observe the time so the student doesn't take more than the specified amount of time to complete the passage.
* Do not correct errors unless the correction is necessary for the student to keep reading the passage. If the student can't read a word within about two seconds, say the word and mark it as an error.

Note: Have students read from the first star to the second star as part of the specified fluency checkout. Additional text is provided that is not included in the rate criterion of each passage.

Decoding errors consist of misidentification, word omissions, line-skipping, and word additions. Self-corrects and rereading words may also be counted as errors if either occurs more than twice while reading the passage.

Criterion: The student must read the entire selection within the time period specified and must make no more than the specified numbers of errors. These criteria are listed at the top of the Fluency: Rate/Accuracy Checkout Recording Form on pages 80 and 81.

Use the Individual Fluency Checkout Charts on page 79 to record stars earned during fluency checkouts. Two stars are earned when the student successfully completes the fluency checkout the first time and 1 star is earned if the checkout is completed on the second attempt.

Recording the Fluency Checkouts

Beginning with lesson 5, the students are given individual checkouts for decoding rate and accuracy. Instructions for administering the checkouts appear in the Presentation Books.

You may use the chart on pages 80 and 81 to record the students' performance on the checkouts. Make a copy of the chart, and then enter the students' names on the left side of the chart, under the heading "names." The students' scores are recorded in the boxes under the appropriate lesson number. Students can earn a maximum of 2 stars for each checkout and 8 for each 20-lesson period.

the talking cat

the girl was gōiñg fōr a walk. shē met a fat cat. "can cats talk?" the girl said.

the cat said, "I can talk, but I do not talk to girls. I talk to dogs."

the girl did not līke that cat. "I do not līke cats that will not talk to mē."

the cat said, "I will not talk to girls."

the girl said, "I do not līke that cat. and I do not givₑ fish cākₑ to cats I do not līke."

the cat said, "I līke fish cākₑ, sō I will talk to this girl."

sō the girl and the cat ātₑ the fish cākₑ.

the end *

* the dog and the bath

wē had a big dog. her nāme was sal. this dog līked to run and plāy. this dog did not līke to take a bath.

wē said, "come in, sal. it is tīme to tāke a bath." wē ran after her.

wē said, "sal, if you come back and tāke a bath, you can have some cōrn." but shē did not līke cōrn.

wē said, "if you come back and tāke a bath, you can have some mēat." but shē did not līke mēat.

wē said, "if you come back and tāke a bath, you can rēad a book." *

the big dog cāme back and took a bath. why did sal tāke a bath? shē līked to rēad books. this is the end.

the cow boys have
a jumping meet

the cow boy got on a cow. the other cow boys said, "hō, hō. that is funny."

the cow boy got mad. hē said, "this cow can gō as fast as a hōrse. and shē can jump better than a hōrse."

* the other cow boys said, "nō cow can jump better than mȳ hōrse." sō the cow boys rōde to a crēēk.

the cow boy on the cow said, "let's sēē if a hōrse can jump this crēēk."

"I will trȳ," a cow boy said. his hōrse went up to the crēēk. but then his hōrse stopped. and the cow boy fell in the crēēk.

the cow boy on the cow said, "hō, hō. that hōrse didn't ēven trȳ to jump the crēēk."

the next cow boy said, "mȳ hōrse will trȳ. and mȳ hōrse will flȳ ōver that strēam."*

jill trĪed and trĪed

did jill trȳ to do thiñgs?

did her sister trȳ to do thiñgs?

what did jill do when shē trĪed?

jill said, "I can not rēad a book, but I will trȳ."

what did jill sāy?

* her sister said, "I can not rēad a book, but I will not trȳ."

what did her sister sāy?

sō jill trĪed to rēad and her sister did not trȳ.

now jill is good at rēadiñg. but her sister can not rēad books. her sister can not rĪde a bĪke. her sister can not jump rōpe. and her sister can not rēad books. but her sister can do some thiñg better than jill. her sister can rēally crȳ.

this is the end. *

the boy asked why

a boy nāmed don līked to ask why. his mother tōld him to stāy in the yard. hē asked, "why?" sō shē tōld him why. shē said, "wē will ēat soon." what did shē sāy?

don dug a big hōle in the yard. his brother said, "you must not dig hōles in the yard."

don asked, "why?" sō his brother tōld him. his brother said, "hōles māke the yard look bad." what did his brother sāy?

don got a can of whīte pāint. "I will pāint my bīke whīte," hē said. sō hē got the pāint brush and started to pāint his bīke.

his sister asked, "what are you doing?"

don answered, "pāinting my bīke whīte."

what did the boy sāy?

mōre to come *

the farmer sōld his buttons

whāt did the farmer līke?

wherₑ did he havₑ his best buttons?

whāt did the man want to buȳ from the farmer?

the man kept buȳīng buttons and the farmer kept sellīng them. the man said, "now you havₑ fīvₑ buttons. I want to buȳ that pink button." so the farmer took off his pink button and sōld it to the man.

* then the man wanted to buȳ the farmer's yellōw button. so the farmer sōld the yellōw button to the man.

the man said, "you still havₑ thrēē buttons. I will buȳ them."

(Continued)*

so the farmer took off the three buttons. but when his pants had no mōre buttons, his pants fell down. what did they do?

the farmer said, "mȳ pants fell down bēcause I sōld the buttons that held up mȳ pants." what did he sāy?

so now the farmer has monēy, but he has no buttons to kēep his pants up. how will he kēep his pants up?

this is the end. *

the bug in the ball meets a girl

a small bug had a home in a ball. he said, "I hope I can stay in this ball. I like it here."

he went to sleep in the ball. he was having a good dream. he was dreaming of a fine party. then he sat up. the ball was rolling. "what is going on?" he called.

he looked from the little hole in the ball and saw a tall girl. she was rolling the ball on the floor.

"what are you doing?" he asked. "this is my home. stop rolling it on the floor."

the girl picked up the ball and looked at the small bug. then she dropped the ball. "oh," she cried, "there is a bug in my ball. I hate bugs."

(Continued)

the ball hit the flōōr. it went up. then it went down. then it went up. the bug was getting sick.

"stop that," he called. "I dōn't lIke a hōme that gōes up and down."

the tall girl bent down and looked at the bug. she said, "this is mȳ ball. so go awāy."

the small bug looked up at the girl and started to crȳ.

mōre to come *

*the dog loves to rēₐd,
rēₐd, rēₐd

a dog that could talk livₑd with a tall man. the dog took a book from the tāblₑ. the dog said, "this book is what I nēēd, nēēd, nēēd. I love to rēₐd, rēₐd, rēₐd."

the tall man cāmₑ in and said, "I look, look, look, but I cannot sēē mȳ book, book, book."

then the man said, "mȳ book was on the tāblₑ."

the dog said, "the book was on the tāblₑ, but I took it from the tāblₑ."

the tall man yellₑd at the dog.*

he said, "you must not tākₑ mȳ book from the tāblₑ."

she said, "do you want to plāy ball, ball, ball in the hall, hall, hall?"

(Continued)

"yes, yes," the man said.

the dog kicked the ball far, far, far down the hall. when the man ran after the ball, the dog took the book and hid it.

then she said, "let the man look, look, look. he will never find his book, book, book."

the end

* <u>walter kicks the ball</u>

walter was ready to kick the ball. the boys and girls on the sīde of the lot werₑ sāyiñg, "dōn't let walter kick."

but walter did kick. another boy held the ball. a tall boy from the other tēam almōst got to the ball, but walter kickₑd the ball just in tīmₑ. the ball went līkₑ a shot. it went past the end of the lot. it went ōver a tall wall that was next to the lot. it almōst hit a car that was on the strēēt.

the boys on walter's tēam lookₑd at walter. the boys on the other tēam lookₑd at walter. one boy from the other tēam said, "that ball went all the wāy ōver the wall. I did not think * that a small boy could kick a ball so far."

(Continued)

the boys and girls on the sīde
of the lot chēēred. "that's the wāy
to kick, walter," they called.

now walter's tēam nēēded one
mōre scōre to win the gāme.

mōre to come

* jill's mouse

jill had a pet mouse. her mouse
was little and pink. jill got a
little box for her little mouse. then
she went to her mother and said,
"look what I have. I have a pet
mouse in this box."

her mother jumped up. her
mother said, "get that mouse out of
this house."

jill said, "but I want to keep
this mouse."

her mother said, "you can't keep
that mouse in this house. I don't
like that mouse."

jill asked, "would you let me
keep this mouse in the yard? then
the mouse would not be around you." *

"yes," her mother said, "but keep
that mouse out of this house."

so jill took the box and went to
the yard. she said, "I will make a
house for this mouse." so she piled
some grass around the box.

(Continued)

now jill is happy and her mother
is happy. and the mouse is happy.
why was jill happy?
why was her mother happy?
why was the mouse happy?
the end

* the magic pouch

what was insIde the pouch?

how many yēars had the elf lived in the pouch?

the little girl said to herself, "should I ōpen this pouch?" she looked at the pouch. then slōwly she ōpened it. out jumped a little elf, no bigger than your foot. the girl's hound went, "owwwww." then the elf jumped all around the room. he jumped on the tāble and on the flōōr. then he ran up one wall and down the other wall. he ēven ran around the hound. "owwwww," the hound yelled.

"I'm out. I'm out," the elf shouted. "I lived in that pouch a *
thousand yēars and now I'm out."

at last the girl's hound stopped gōing "owwwww." the elf sat on the tāble and said, "I thank you very much. plēase tāke the magic pouch.

(Continued)

but be cāreful. when you are good, the pouch will be good to you. but when you are bad, the pouch will be bad to you.

more to come

the pet gōat

a girl got a pet gōat. ʃhe liked to go runniñg with her pet gōat. ʃhe plāyed with her gōat in her houʃe. ʃhe plāyed with the gōat in her yard.

but the gōat did some thiñgs that made the girl's dad mad. the gōat ate thiñgs. he ate cans and he ate canes. he ate pans and he ate panes. he ēven ate capes and caps.

one dāy her dad said, "that gōat must go. he ēats too many thiñgs."

the girl said, "dad, if you let the gōat stāy with us, I will see that he stops ēatiñg all those thiñgs."

her dad said, "we will trȳ it."

so the gōat stāyed and the girl made him stop ēatiñg cans and canes and caps and capes. *

but one dāy a car robber came to the girl's houʃe. he saw a big red car nēar the houʃe and said, "I will stēal that car."

(Continued)

he ran to the car and started to ōpen the dōōr.

the girl and the gōat were plāyiñg in the back yard. they did not see the car robber.

Fluency: Rate/Accuracy Checkouts

the small cloud must help

the wind was blowing the small cloud away from his father and mother. the small cloud couldn't ēven see them any more. "I am so sad that I will crȳ," the cloud said. but what do you think happened? when the cloud trīed to crȳ, no tēars came out. that made the cloud ēven sadder.

he said, "I am so small that I can't ēven make tēars."

just then someone called, "help, help."

the little cloud looked down. there was a small dēēr and a mother dēēr. and nēar them was a big forest fire. that small dēēr and the mother dēēr were trapped. "help, help," they called.

(Continued)*

* the little cloud said to himself, "I must get help." then he called, "mom and dad, come ōver here and make some rāin on the forest." but the mother cloud and the father cloud werе too far awāy. they couldn't hēar the little cloud.

"what will I do?" the little cloud asked himself. "if I could make rāin, I could help those dēēr. but I am too small."

the fire was getting bigger all the time. now it was all around the two dēēr. the small cloud said, "I must get mȳ mother and father."

but every time the small cloud started to flōat one wāy, the wind took him back. the small cloud looked down at the two dēēr. then the cloud said, "I am the ōnly one who can help those dēēr. so I will do what I can."

more to come *

sandy fīnds the trāin car

When sandy counted the cars on her wāy to school, there were one hundred cars in the trāin. when she counted the cars after school, there were ninety-nine cars. one car was missing.

sandy said, "I must think about this. there were fifty red cars and fifty yellōw cars. but now there are not fifty red cars. one red car is missing."

sandy walked next to the rāil rōad track.

soon she came to a shed. there were rāil rōad tracks that led to the shed. sandy said to herself, "I will fīnd out what is in that shed."

(Continued)

* so sandy follōwed the tracks to the shed.

she looked inside the shed and saw a red trāin car standiñg on the tracks. the car dōōr was ōpen. sandy looked around. no one was around. so sandy ran ōver to the dōōr of the red car and looked inside. the car was filled with tv sets.

she said to herself, "I found the car with the tv sets."

sandy was all set to run back to tell someone that she had found the missiñg car. but just then there was a sound nēar her. it was the sound of foot steps.

more to come *

* thank you, sandy

sandy and the others were near the shed. the cop said, "the rest of you wait here. I'll go inside that shed and see what's going on."

so they waited as the cop went into the shed. as soon as the cop was in the shed, big bill said, "I've got work to do. I'm leaving."

"you better stay here," one of the men said. big bill didn't answer. bill just gave sandy a mean look.

sandy looked at the shed and waited. then she saw some men start to come from the shed. they all had their hands up. the cop was walking behind them. *

* the fox wants a cone

a little girl was sitting in the woods. she had an ice crēam cone. she was sitting on a log, ēating her ice crēam cone.

a slȳ fox was looking at her. that fox was thinking. "I will con that girl. I will con her into giving me her cone."

so the slȳ fox ran up to the girl. then he fell ōver and began to shout, "help me, help me. mȳ mouth is on fire. give me something cool for mȳ mouth."

"close your eyes and ōpen your mouth," the girl said.

the slȳ fox was thinking, "hō, hō, I conned that girl out of her cone."

when the fox closed his eyes, he *did not get a cone in his mouth. he got a drink of cōld water.

"there," the girl said. "that should make your mouth cool."

"no, no," the fox shouted. "mȳ mouth nēēds something cōlder than that water."

the girl said, "close your eyes and ōpen your mouth."

the fox said to himself, "this time I will con her out of her cone."

but he did not con her out of a cone. he conned her out of a bit of ice. she dropped the ice into his mouth. then she said, "now your mouth must fēēl cool."

"no, no," the fox yelled. "I nēēd a cone."

* don has Super fun

Who gave don the dime?

Where did he tape the dime?

Was he doing good things?

did don mope after he became a super man?

don was hopping around the store in his cap and his cape. he was hitting the walls and making holes. he was having a lot of fun.

all at once he stopped. he said, "I will go outside and show what a super man I am."

When don left the store, he didn't open the door. he ran into the door. "Crash."

Some boys were standing outside the store. They said, "look at that funny man in a cap and a cape."

★ don said, "I am no funny man. I am a super man."

* Sid Worked in a Seed Shop

Sid had a job. he worked in a seed shop. That shop had lots of little plants.

The boss of the shop had a bad leg. So she walked with a cane. When she was not walking with her cane, she left her cane in a big can near the door.

One day the boss said, "I must hop in the truck and go to the other side of town. You stay here and take care of the shop."

So the boss got her cane from the can and went to the truck. When she got in her truck, she said, "There is a pile of notes on the table. Take care of them."★

* Dan the Teacher

A girl named Ann had a dog. The dog was named Dan. One day Dan went to school with Ann.

The teacher said, "Ann, take that dog out of this school. Schools are for boys and girls. Schools are not for dogs."

Ann said, "But this dog is very smart. He likes to read and he likes to add."

The teacher said, "I will let that dog stay, but if he makes a sound, I will make him leave."

So the dog sat down to read a book to himself. The boys and girls worked with the teacher.

But then the teacher was called out of the room.

One boy said, "We do not have a teacher ★ now."

* The Ugly Duckling

There once was a mother duck who found a big egg. She said, "I will put this egg with my other eggs." And so she did.

Soon all of the eggs hatched. The little eggs hatched and the big egg that she found hatched. What do you think came out of the big egg? A funny-looking duckling. He was big, and he kept falling down when he tried to walk.

The other ducklings called him names. "You are ugly," they said. "You are an ugly duckling."

The ugly duckling was sad. None of the other ducklings would play with him. They just called him names. "Boy, are you ever an ugly duckling," they would say.

The ★ ugly duckling said to himself, "I am so ugly and nobody likes me."

* Boo Goes to the Castle

The five mean ghosts had made Boo leave the old house. When Boo was walking to town, he found a talking frog. The frog was near a stream. But the frog was not really a frog. It was a king. A monster had cast a spell on the king and turned him into a frog.

"I will help you," Boo said. "Just tell me where the monster stays."

The frog said, "The monster is in my castle. That castle is on the other side of town."

"You wait here," Boo said. "I will be back."

Boo floated up into the sky. He floated over the town like a bird. Soon he came to the castle ★ on the other side of town.

* Boo Casts Some Spells

The ghosts had found words on the side of the rod. The ghost who was holding the rod said, "I can't read." Then he looked at the other mean ghosts. "Who can read these words?" he asked.

"Not me," they all said. Then the three ghosts looked at Boo.

"You can read," one ghost said. "So read these words and tell us how to turn you into a leaf."

Boo said, "Hand me the rod and I will do the best I can."

So the ghost handed the rod to Boo, and Boo looked at the words on the rod. Then Boo held the rod and said, "Bit bite, ben bean."

Nothing happened to Boo, but the other ghosts began to smile. One ghost said, "I don't feel mean anymore."

Another ghost said, "I feel ★ like playing games with the boys and girls in town."

* Ott Tells Lies

When the mean boys tried to take the bottle from Carla, she rubbed the bottle and Ott appeared.

Ott said, "Oh, master Carla, what can I do for you?"

Carla said, "Give those boys a spanking."

"Yes, master," Ott said. He sounded smart, but he didn't know how to give the boys a spanking. He could only remember the word banking.

"Well," Carla said at last, "are you going to give them a spanking?"

"Yes," Ott said. "A spanking it will be."

Ott waved his hands. Suddenly, Carla, Ott, and the three boys were in a bank. They were banking.

Carla said, "What kind of a genie are you?"

The boys said, "Let's get out of here," and they began to run from the bank as fast as they could go.

Ott was very sad. He said, ★ "Carla, I am a very old genie."

* Carla Reads the Genie Book

Carla and Ott were in Rome. Ott had just made something happen the right way. He had wished for a window pane, and the pane came.

"I think I can get us out of here," Ott said. "But maybe I should call for help. I think I can do that now."

"All right," Carla said. "Call for help." Ott folded his arms and began to say things to himself. Then something began to fly across the sky. It began to dive at Ott. "Splat." It was a big wet, fat fish.

Carla began to laugh. Then she said, "I don't think you're a genie yet."

"You are right," Ott said. Then he held up a big book. "This is my school book," he said. "It tells you how to do things like a genie. Maybe we can read the book and find out how to ★ go home."

* Will Carla Take the Genie Vow?

The day had come for everyone in school to take a vow to be a genie. The old genie came to class that day. She had a ring for every new genie.

Before she gave out the rings, she stood in front of the class and said, "Today is your last day in this school. You have worked hard and now you are ready to leave. You are ready to take your place as a genie. But before you take your vow, remember this. It is not easy to be a genie. You must forget about the things that you want to do. You must think about your master. You must do only what your master wants you to do. Not all of you will have good masters. But once you take the genie vow, you must do what genies have done for ★ thousands and thousands of years."

Kim Moves Her Stuff in a Van

Kim was really mad. After the man left Kim with a set of false teeth, Kim picked up the phone book and tossed it out of the window. She shouted, "That book gets me in a lot of trouble."

A boy was passing by Kim's house. He stopped and picked up the phone book. He said, "Is this your book?"

"I just tossed it away," Kim said. "I can't find anything in it."

"What do you want to find?" the boy asked.

"I need a van to take my things to the other side of town."

"Here," the boy said. He walked over to Kim. He had already found the right place in the phone book. "Why don't you call this number? It says that they have very fast service every day."

So Kim called the number. She said to the ★ woman who answered the phone, "I don't want a vane."

* Flame the Snake Is a Sneak

Flame the snake was looking for something to eat. The turtle said, "No, I have not seen any frogs around here."

Flame smiled and started to slide back into the weeds. Then that snake stopped and said, "I will be back."

The turtle said to himself, "I don't like that snake. I think she is a sneak. I think I will leave." The turtle walked into the pond and began to swim around. Then the frog came over to him. The frog said, "What did Flame say to you?"

The turtle said, "She said that she wanted something to eat."

The frog asked, "Did she say what she wanted to eat?"

"Yes," the turtle said. "She told me that she wanted to eat a frog."

"That is bad," the frog said. "That is very, very bad." The frog jumped from the pond and sat ★ on an old log.

* The Rabbit and the Turtle

All of the other animals wanted to see the turtle beat the rabbit in a race. The rabbit had told everybody that she would stop telling how fast she was if the turtle beat her. But the rabbit seemed far too fast for the turtle. The rabbit went flying over the path and over the stream. Soon she was at the hill. She stopped to look back. All she could see was a cloud of dust. "Ho, ho," she said. "That turtle must be a mile behind me. He cannot win this race."

So the rabbit sat down under a tree. She closed her eyes and leaned back. And the first thing you know she was sound asleep.

The turtle didn't stop when the rabbit got far ahead of him. The turtle kept going as fast as he could go. He just kept going and going.   He said to himself, "I'll just keep on going, ★ and I'll beat that rabbit."

* The Prince and the Tramp

There once was a prince. The prince always dressed in fine clothes. He had a gold crown and a long robe and red shoes. When the prince walked down the streets of the city, everybody would say, "We love the prince. He is so handsome."

When the prince was hungry, people would bring food to him. Then the prince would say to himself, "Everybody loves me."

When the prince was tired of walking, people would give him a horse to ride.

One day the prince met a tramp. This tramp did not have a gold crown, or a long robe, or red shoes. This tramp did not have any shoes. He had an old shirt with holes in it. But that tramp looked just like the prince.

The tramp said, "How strange. You look just like me."

The prince said, "Let us have some fun. I will dress like you, and you will dress like ★ me."

* Jean Looks for Food

Jean was dreaming about a strange place. She was at the mountain in the land of peevish pets. And she was very hungry. She said, "I wish I had something to eat, and I wish the wizard was here."

Just then the wizard appeared. He said, "You may eat all you want, but remember this rule: Red food is good to eat. See if you can say that rule."

Jean said, "Red food is good to eat."

The wizard said, "Good remembering."

Jean said, "I will remember that rule. But what and when . . . ."

The wizard was gone again. Jean said to herself, "That is strange. Every time I say 'But what and when,' the wizard goes away."

Jean looked around and found lots of food. There was food on the ground. There was food on the side of the mountain. There was a bowl of yellow ice cream right in front of her.   Should she eat that yellow ice cream?

How do you know?

Tell Jean the rule before she tries to eat that ice cream. ★

A Funny Animal Appears

The wizard told Jean a rule for getting her hair back. Tell Jean that rule.

Jean started to ask the wizard, "But what and when . . . ."

But the wizard disappeared before she could ask the question. Jean said, "I think I'll get my hair back." Jean clapped her hands. So did she get her hair back?

Jean felt her head. Her hair was back. She ran to the lake and looked at herself in the water. Her hair was back, but it was striped again.

She said, "Oh, well. I would rather have striped hair than be bald."

Just then a big, funny-looking animal came out of the lake. Part of that animal looked like a horse, and part of that animal looked like a monkey. The animal walked up to Jean and said, "I can help you get out of this place. I know all sixteen rules."

"Good," Jean said, "Teach me the rules I don't know."

The funny animal said, "Here's a good rule: All dusty paths lead to the mountain."

"No," Jean said. ★

* Leaving the Land of Peevish Pets

Jean had found out fifteen rules. The last rule she found out told about making the wizard disappear. She needed only one more rule. So she sat down and began to think. Suddenly, she jumped up. She said, "I've got it. Every time I needed help, the wizard appeared. I think that's the rule. I'll find out." She stood up and yelled, "I need help."

Suddenly, the wizard appeared. Jean said, "I think I know all of the rules. I know how to make you appear. Here's the rule: If you want the wizard to appear, call for help."

"Good," the wizard said.

Then Jean said, "So now I can leave this land of peevish pets."

"That is right," the wizard said. "You have found out all the rules. So you may leave. Just close your eyes."

Jean closed her eyes. Suddenly, she felt something licking her face.

She opened her eyes. She was in bed. Her mom and dad were standing near the bed, and there was a puppy on the bed. He was licking Jean's face. ★

Curriculum-Based *Assessments*

Lesson 20

Introducing the Assessment

The Lesson 20 curriculum-based assessment should be introduced after the students complete all work on lesson 20 and before they begin work on lesson 21. To introduce the assessment, you will need an Assessment Book and a pencil for each student. Use the following script:

1. (Direct the students to clear their desks and make sure that each student has a pencil.)

2. You will be taking some assessments on what you have learned. I will give each of you an Assessment Book. Do not open the book until I tell you.

3. (Pass out the Assessment Books.)

   Now look at the back cover of your Assessment Book. The back cover shows what the assessments will be like. You can see that they are a lot like your worksheets. Now turn to page 16. ✔

4. Everybody, touch the picture for item 1. ✔
   - Now touch the sentence and follow along as I read it. ✔
   - **The cat has a blank.** You have to figure out which word goes in the blank. Read the words under the sentence and get ready to tell me which word goes in the blank. (Wait.) Everybody, which word goes in the blank? (Signal.) *Hat.* Yes, **hat.**
   - Everybody, circle the word **hat.** ✔

5. Now touch the sentence above item 2. ✔
   - Follow along as I read the story sentence. **A cow boy was sad.** Now touch item 2 and follow along as I read it. ✔
   - **A blank boy was sad.** You have to figure out which word goes in the blank. Everybody, read the words under the sentence and get ready to tell me which word goes in the blank. (Wait.) Everybody, which word goes in the blank? (Signal.) *Cow.* Yes, **cow.**
   - Everybody, circle the word **cow.** ✔

6. You will answer most of the items in your Assessment Book like you answered these sample items. For each item, you must circle the correct answer.

Administering the Assessment

Use the following script to administer the assessment:

1. Everybody, open your Assessment Book to page 2. ✔

2. You're going to take the assessment on your own. Let's go over the things you're going to do.

3. Look at items 1 and 2. ✔
- For items 1 and 2, you will look at the picture and then circle the words that go in the blanks.

4. Now look at items 3 and 4. ✔
- For items 3 and 4, you will read the story and then circle the words that go in the blanks.

5. Now look at items 5 and 6. ✔
- For items 5 and 6, you will read the story and then circle the words that go in the blanks.

6. Begin the assessment now. There is no time limit. When you are finished, close your Assessment Book and look up at me.

Grading the Assessment

Use the answer key below to grade the assessments. If an answer is correct, mark it with a *C*. If an answer is wrong, mark it with an *X*. After you have marked all the answers, count up the number of *correct* answers and enter the score at the top of the assessment.

Answer Key

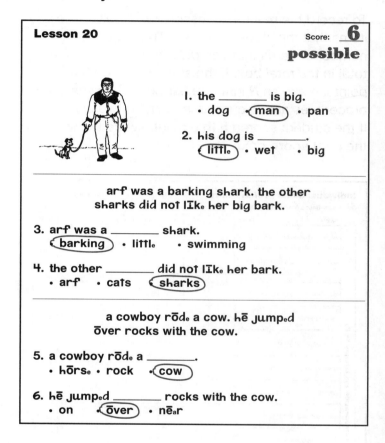

Recording Individual Results

Individual assessment results should be recorded on the Individual Skills Profile Chart, which is located on page 83. The first column of the chart lists the assessed skills. The remaining columns indicate which assessment items measure those skills. For example, the skill "writing the names of pictured objects" is measured by items 1 and 2 on the assessment for lesson 20.

To record the results for lesson 20, simply circle any items that the student missed. Then count up the number of items that you did *not* circle and enter the total in the *total* box. If the student scored 0 to 4 points, make an *R* in the *retest* box. (Reassessment procedures are discussed in the next two sections.) If the student scored 5 to 6 points, write the score in the **final score** box.

Individual Skills Profile Chart

Name: **Sample**

Curriculum-Based Assessments Lessons 20-160

Skills	Tests	20	40	60	80	100	120	140	160
writing the names of pictured objects		1 2							
answering literal questions about a text		3 4 5 ⑥	3 6	4 8	5 8	6 7 8	7 10	10	6
identifying literal cause and effect			4			9	9		7
recalling details and events								1 2	1 2
following written directions			1 2	1 2 3	1 2 3	1 2 3	3 4		
applying rules									1 2
predicting narrative outcomes			5	5	7	10	8	9	10
inferring causes and effects				6				8	
inferring story details and events					6				8
using rules to classify objects						4 5	5	4 5	4 5
completing written deductions								3	3
interpreting a character's feelings				7				6	
interpreting a character's motives					4		6	7	9
Total		**5**							
Retest									
FINAL SCORE		**5**							

Comprehension and Literary Skills

Remedial Exercises

Students who scored 0 to 4 points on the assessment should be given remedial help. After the regular reading period is over, assemble these students and present the following exercises. The students will need their marked Assessment Books, but will not need pencils.

EXERCISE 1   Picture Comprehension

1. Everybody, open your Assessment Book to page 2. ✔

2. Everybody, touch the picture. ✔
- Now touch item 1. ✔

   Item 1 tells about the picture. Get ready to read item **1.**

3. Get ready. (Tap for each word.) *The blank is big.*

   Look at the picture and get ready to tell me who is big. (Pause.)

   Everybody, who is big? (Signal.) *The man.*

4. Now touch item 2. ✔

- Item 2 tells about the picture. Get ready to read item 2.

5. Get ready. (Tap for each word.) *His dog is blank.*
- Look at the picture and get ready to tell me what his dog is like. (Pause.)
- Everybody, what is his dog like? (Signal.) *Little.*

EXERCISE 2   Story Reading

1. Everybody, touch the first story. ✔
- Get ready to read the first sentence. (Tap for each word.) *Arf was a barking shark.*

2. Everybody, what kind of shark was Arf? (Signal.) *A barking shark.*

3. Get ready to read the next sentence. (Tap for each word.) *The other sharks did not like her big bark.*

4. Everybody, who did not like Arf's bark? (Signal.) *The other sharks.*

5. Everybody, touch the next story. ✔
- Get ready to read the first sentence. (Tap for each word.) *A cow boy rode a cow.*

6. Everybody, what did the cow boy ride? (Signal.) *A cow.*

7. Get ready to read the next sentence. (Tap for each word.) *He jumped over rocks with the cow.*

8. Everybody, what did the cow boy jump over? (Signal.) *Rocks.*

Reassessing the Students

After you have completed the remedial exercises, reassess each student individually. To administer the reassessment, you will need the student's Assessment Book, a blank copy of the Assessment Book, and a red pencil. Assess the student in a corner of the classroom, so that the other students will not overhear the assessment. Give the student the blank copy of the Assessment Book. Say, "Look at page 2. You're going to take this assessment again. Read each item aloud and tell me the answer."

You should use the student's own Assessment Book to grade the reassessment. Use the red pencil to mark each correct answer with a *C* and each incorrect answer with an *X*. Then count one point for each correct answer and write the new score at the top of the page. Finally, revise the Individual Skills Profile Chart by drawing an *X* over any items the student missed on the reassessment and writing the new score in the *final score* box. The chart should now show which items the student missed on the initial assessment and which items the student missed on the reassessment. Page 82 of this Handbook shows a completed Individual Skills Profile Chart.

Recording Group Results

After you have completely filled in the Individual Skills Profile Chart, you should fill in the Group Point Chart, which appears on page 85 of this Handbook. Make a copy of the chart, and then enter the students' names on the left side of the chart. The students' scores are recorded in the boxes under the appropriate lesson number.

First record the points that each student earned on the individual reading checkouts. Look at the Individual Checkout Chart. Count up the number of stars the student earned on the checkouts for lessons 5 to 20 and enter the total (up to 8) in the *left* side of the appropriate box. Then enter the student's final Lesson 20 assessment score in the *right* side of the box.

Group Point Chart

Lessons	20	40	60	80	100	120	140	160	check-outs	tests
Highest possible number of stars / Highest possible benchmark test score	8 / 6	8 / 6	8 / 8	8 / 8	8 / 10	8 / 10	8 / 10	8 / 10	64	68
Lupe Baco	6 / 5									
Tatsu Boki	8 / 5									
Don Clark	7 / 5									

Page 85 of this Handbook shows a completed Group Point chart.

Assessed Skills

The Lesson 20 curriculum-based assessment measures student mastery of the following skills:

- writing the names of pictured objects (items 1–2)
- answering literal questions about a text (items 3–6)

Lesson 40

Administering the Assessment

The Lesson 40 curriculum-based assessment should be administered after the students complete all work on lesson 40 and before they begin work on lesson 41. To administer the assessment, you will need a Assessment Book and a pencil for each student. Use the following script:

1. (Direct the students to clear their desks and make sure that each student has a pencil.)

2. Now you're going to take another assessment in your Assessment Book. Do not open the book until I tell you.

3. (Pass out the Assessment Books.)

4. Everybody, open your Assessment Book to page 3. ✔

5. You're going to take the assessment on your own. Let's go over the things you're going to do.

6. Look at items 1 and 2. ✔
   • For items 1 and 2, you will do what the instructions tell you to do.

7. Now look at items 3 through 6. ✔
   • For items 3 through 6, you will read the story and then circle the correct answers.

8. Begin the assessment now. There is no time limit. When you are finished, close your Assessment Book and look up at me.

Grading the Assessment

Use the answer key in the next column to grade each assessment. If an answer is correct, mark it with a C. If an answer is wrong, mark it with an X. Count up the number of correct answers and enter the score at the top of the assessment.

Answer Key

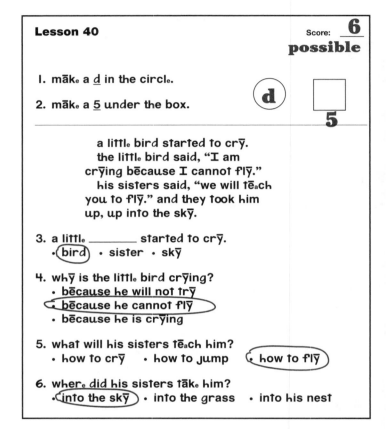

Recording Individual Results

After you have graded the assessments, enter the assessment results on each student's Individual Skills Profile Chart. Circle any items that the student missed, and then count up the number of items that you did *not* circle and enter the total in the *total* box. If the student scored 0 to 4 points, make an *R* in the *reassessment* box. If the student scored 5 to 6 points, write the score in the *final score* box.

Remedial Exercises

Students who scored 0 to 4 points on the assessment should be given remedial help. After the regular reading period is over, assemble these students and present the following exercises. The students will need their marked Assessment Books, but not pencils.

EXERCISE 1   Following Instructions

1. Everybody, open your Assessment Book to page 3. ✔

2. Touch item 1. ✔
- Get ready to read item 1. (Tap for each word.) *Make d in the circle.*

3. Everybody, what will you make in the circle? (Signal.) *D.*
- Where will you make d? (Signal.) *In the circle.*

4. Everybody, touch item 2. ✔
- Get ready to read item 2. (Tap for each word.) *Make a 5 under the box.*

5. Everybody, where will you make a 5? (Signal.) *Under the box.*
- What will you make under the box? (Signal.) *A 5.*

EXERCISE 2   Story Reading

1. Everybody, touch the story. ✔

2. Get ready to read the first sentence. (Tap for each word.) *A little bird started to cry.*
- Everybody, who started to cry? (Signal.) *A little bird.*

3. Get ready to read the next sentence. (Tap for each word.) *The little bird said, "I am crying because I cannot fly."*
- Everybody, what can't the little bird do? (Signal.) *Fly.*
- So what is the little bird doing? (Signal.) *Crying.*

4. Everybody, get ready to read the next sentence. (Tap for each word.) *His sisters said, "We will teach you to fly."*
- Everybody, who will teach him to fly? (Signal.) *His sisters.*

5. Everybody, get ready to read the last sentence. (Tap for each word.) *And they took him up, up into the sky.*
- Everybody, who took the little bird up, up? (Signal.) *His sisters.*
- Everybody, what did they go into? (Signal.) *The sky.*

Reassessing the Students

After you have completed the remedial exercises, reassess each student individually. To administer the reassessment, you will need the student's Assessment Book, a blank copy of the Assessment Book, and a red pencil. Assess the student in a corner of the classroom, so that the other students will not overhear the assessment. Give the student the blank copy of the Assessment Book. Say "Look at page 3. You're going to take this assessment again. Read each item aloud and tell me the answer."

You should use the student's own Assessment Book to grade the reassessment. Use the red pencil to mark each correct answer with a *C* and each incorrect answer with an *X*. Then count one point for each correct answer and write the new score at the top of the page.

After grading the reassessment, revise the student's Individual Skills Profile Chart by drawing an x over any items the student missed on the reassessment. Then write the new score in the *final score* box.

Recording Group Results

Look at the Individual Checkout Chart and count up the number of stars each student earned on the checkouts for lessons 25 to 40. Then enter the total in the *left* side of the appropriate boxes on the Group Point Chart. Enter the students' final assessment scores in the *right* side of each box.

Assessed Skills

The Lesson 40 curriculum-based assessment measures student mastery of the following skills:

- answering literal questions about a text (items 3 and 6)
- identifying literal cause and effect (item 4)
- following written directions (items 1–2)
- predicting narrative outcomes (item 5)

Lesson 60

Administering the Assessment

The Lesson 60 curriculum-based assessment should be administered after the students complete all work on lesson 60 and before they begin work on lesson 61. To administer the assessment, you will need a Assessment Book and a pencil for each student. Use the following script:

1. (Direct the students to clear their desks and make sure that each student has a pencil.)

2. Now you're going to take another assessment in your Assessment Book. Do not open the book until I tell you.

3. (Pass out the Assessment Books.)

4. Everybody, open your Assessment Book to page 4. ✔

5. You're going to take the assessment on your own. Let's go over the things you're going to do.

6. Look at items 1 through 3. ✔
• For items 1 through 3, you will do what the instructions tell you to do.

7. Now look at items 4 through 8. ✔
• For items 4 through 8, you will read the story and then circle the correct answers.

8. Begin the assessment now. There is no time limit. When you are finished, close your Assessment Book and look up at me.

Grading the Assessment

Use the answer key in the next column to grade each assessment. If an answer is correct, mark it with a C. If an answer is wrong, mark it with an X. Count up the number of *correct* answers and enter the score at the top of the assessment.

Answer Key

Lesson 60   Score: **8** possible

she is fall.

1. make a box around the word **is**.

who are you?

2. circle the word **who**.

I am happy.

3. make a line under the word **happy**.

an elf gave a little girl a magic pouch. the elf said, "when you are good, the pouch will be good to you. but when you are bad, the pouch will be bad to you."

the girl picked up the pouch. she said, "I have been good. let's see if this magic pouch will be good to me."

she reached inside the pouch and found some gold. "I'm rich," she shouted. the girl was happy.

4. the elf gave the girl a _____ pouch.
• magic   • gold   • good

5. what will happen when the girl is bad?
• the pouch will be good to her.
• the elf will take the pouch back.
• the pouch will be bad to her.

6. why was the pouch good to the girl?
• because she was good
• because she was bad
• because the elf was bad

7. why was the girl happy?
• because she was sad
• because she was rich
• because she was an elf

8. what did the girl shout?
• "I'm rich!"   • "I'm good!"   • "I'm bad!"

Recording Individual Results

After you have graded the assessments, enter the assessment results on each student's Individual Skills Profile Chart. Circle any items that the student missed, and then count up the number of items that you did *not* circle and enter the total in the *total* box. If the student scored 0 to 6 points, make an *R* in the *reassessment* box. If the student scored 7 to 8 points, write the score in the *final score* box.

Remedial Exercises

Students who scored 0 to 6 points on the assessment should be given remedial help. After the regular reading period is over, assemble these students and present the following exercises. The students will need their marked Assessment Books, but not pencils.

EXERCISE 1   Following Directions

1. Everybody, open your Assessment Book to page 4. ✔

2. Touch the box above item 1. ✔
- Get ready to read the sentence in the box. (Tap for each word.) *She is tall.*

3. Now touch item 1. ✔
- Get ready to read item 1. (Tap for each word.) *Make a box around the word is.*

4. Everybody, what will you make around the word is? (Signal.) *A box.*
- Where will you make **a box?** (Signal.) *Around the word is.*

5. Everybody, touch the box above item 2. ✔
- Get ready to read the sentence in the box. (Tap for each word.) *Who are you?*

6. Now touch item 2. ✔
- Get ready to read item 2. (Tap for each word.) *Circle the word who.*

7. Everybody, what will you do to the word **who?** (Signal.) *Circle it.*

8. Everybody, touch the box above item 3. ✔
- Get ready to read the sentence in the box. (Tap for each word.) *I am happy.*

9. Everybody, touch item 3. ✔
- Get ready to read item 3. (Tap for each word.) *Make a line under the word happy.*
- Everybody, what will you do to the word **happy?** (Signal.) *Make a line under it.*

EXERCISE 2 Story Reading

1. Everybody, touch the story. ✔

2. Get ready to read the first sentence. (Tap for each word.) *An elf gave a little girl a magic pouch.*
- Everybody, what kind of pouch did the elf give her? (Signal.) *A magic pouch.*

3. Get ready to read the next sentence. (Tap for each word.) *The elf said, "When you are good, the pouch will be good to you."*
- Everybody, what will happen when the girl is good? (Signal.) *The pouch will be good to her.*

4. Everybody, get ready to read the next sentence. (Tap for each word.) *"But when you are bad, the pouch will be bad to you."*
- Everybody, what will happen when the girl is bad? (Signal.) *The pouch will be bad to her.*

5. I'm going to call on different students to read a sentence. Everybody, follow along and point to the words. If you hear a mistake, raise your hand.

6. (Call on a student.) Read the next sentence.

7. (Repeat step 6 for the remaining sentences in the story. After the students finish the story, present the following questions.)

8. Everybody, was the girl good? (Signal.) *Yes.*
- So was the pouch good to her or bad to her? (Signal.) *Good to her.*

9. Everybody, what did the girl find inside the pouch? (Signal.) *Gold.*
- So how did the girl feel? (Signal.) *Happy.*
- Everybody, who shouted "I'm rich?" (Signal.) *The girl.*

Reassessing the Students

After you have completed the remedial exercises, reassess each student individually. To administer the reassessment, you will need the student's Assessment Book, a blank copy of the Assessment Book, and a red pencil. Assess the student in a corner of the classroom, so that the other students will not overhear the assessment. Give the student the blank copy of the Assessment Book. Say, "Look at page 4. You're going to take this assessment again. Read each item aloud and tell me the answer."

You should use the student's own Assessment Book to grade the reassessment. Use the red pencil to mark each correct answer with a *C* and each incorrect answer with an *X*. Then count one point for each correct answer and write the new score at the top of the page.

After grading the reassessment, revise the student's Individual Skills Profile Chart by drawing an *X* over any items the student missed on the reassessment. Then write the new score in the *final score* box.

Recording Group Results

Look at the Individual Checkout Chart and count up the number of stars each student earned on the checkouts for lessons 45 to 60. Then enter the total in the *left* side of the appropriate boxes on the Group Point Chart. Enter the students' final assessment scores in the *right* side of each box.

Assessed Skills

The Lesson 60 curriculum-based assessment measures student mastery of the following skills:

- answering literal questions about a text (items 4 and 8)
- following written directions (items 1–3)
- predicting narrative outcomes (item 5)
- inferring causes and effects (item 6)
- interpreting a character's feelings (item 7)

Lesson 80

Administering the Assessment

The Lesson 80 curriculum-based assessment should be administered after the students complete all work on lesson 80 and before they begin work on lesson 81. To administer the assessment, you will need a Assessment Book and a pencil for each student. Use the following script:

1. (Direct the students to clear their desks and make sure that each student has a pencil.)

2. Now you're going to take another assessment in your Assessment Book. Do not open the book until I tell you.

3. (Pass out the Assessment Books.)

4. Everybody, open your Assessment Book to page 6. ✔

5. You're going to take the assessment on your own. Let's go over the things you're going to do.

6. Look at items 1 through 3. ✔
• For items 1 through 3, you will do what the instructions tell you to do.

7. Now look at items 4 through 8. ✔
• For items 4 through 8, you will read the story and then circle the correct answers.

8. Begin the assessment now. There is no time limit. When you are finished, close your Assessment Book and look up at me.

Grading the Assessment

Use the answer key in the next column to grade each assessment. If an answer is correct, mark it with a *C.* If an answer is wrong, mark it with an *X.* Count up the number of *correct* answers and enter the score at the top of the assessment.

Answer Key

Lesson 80   Score: **8**
                                                 possible

the girl ran home.

I. circle the words that tell who ran home.

sid went to a farm.

2. make a line over the words that tell where sid went.

the boys had fun at the park.
                          X

3. make an x under the word at.

sam liked to make toy cars. so he went to the store and got a toy car kit. his mom said, "that kit has the parts of a car. you have to read and find out how to fit the parts so that they make a car."
      so sam began to read the paper that came with the car kit. then he began to fit the parts to make a car. soon he had a toy car.
      sam said, "now I will get a kite kit."

4. why did sam go to the store?
   • to drive a car
   • to get a toy car kit
   • to read a paper

5. who said, "that kit has the parts of a car"?
   • sam   • the man at the store   • sam's mom

6. what did sam find out from the paper?
   • how to drive the car
   • how to get the car
   • how to make the car

7. what will sam make from his next kit?
   • a car   • a kite   • a kitten

8. what kind of car did sam make?
   • a toy car   • a real car   • a kite car

Recording Individual Results

After you have graded the assessments, enter the assessment results on each student's Individual Skills Profile Chart. Circle any items that the student missed, and then count up the number of items that you did *not* circle and enter the total in the *total* box. If the student scored 0 to 6 points, make an *R* in the *reassessment* box. If the student scored 7 to 8 points, write the score in the *final score* box.

Remedial Exercises

Students who scored 0 to 6 points on the assessment should be given remedial help. After the regular reading period is over, assemble these students and present the following exercises. The students will need their marked Assessment Books, but not pencils.

EXERCISE 1 Following Directions

1. Everybody, open your Assessment Book to page 6. ✔

2. Touch the box above item 1. ✔
   - Get ready to read the sentence in the box. (Tap for each word.) *The girl ran home.*

3. Everybody, who ran home? (Signal.) *The girl.*

4. Now touch item 1. ✔
   - Get ready to read item 1. (Tap for each word.) *Circle the words that tell who ran home.*

5. Everybody, who ran home? (Signal.) *The girl.*
   - So what words will you circle? (Signal.) *The girl.*

6. Everybody, touch the box above item 2. ✔
   - Get ready to read the sentence in the box. (Tap for each word.) *Sid went to a farm.*

7. Everybody, where did Sid go? (Signal.) *To a farm.*

8. Now touch item 2. ✔
   - Get ready to read item 2. (Tap for each word.) *Make a line over the words that tell where Sid went.*

9. Everybody, what words will you make a line over? (Signal.) *To a farm.*

10. Everybody, touch the box above item 3. ✔
    - Get ready to read the sentence in the box. (Tap for each word.) *The boys had fun at the park.*

11. Everybody, touch item 3. ✔
    - Get ready to read item 3. (Tap for each word.) *Make an x under the word at.*

12. Everybody, what word will you make an **x** under? (Signal.) *At*

EXERCISE 2 Story Reading

1. Everybody, touch the story. ✔
- Get ready to read the first sentence. (Tap for each word.) *Sam liked to make toy cars.* Everybody, what did Sam like to make? (Signal.) *Toy cars.*

3. Get ready to read the next sentence. (Tap for each word.) *So he went to the store and got a toy car kit.*
- Everybody, what did Sam get at the store? (Signal.) *A toy car kit.*

4. Everybody, get ready to read the next sentence. (Tap for each word.) *His mom said, "That kit has the parts of a car."*
- Everybody, what did his mom say? (Signal.) *That kit has the parts of a car.*

5. I'm going to call on different students to read a sentence. Everybody, follow along and point to the words. If you hear a mistake, raise your hand.

6. (Call on a student.) Read the next sentence.

7. (Repeat step 6 for the remaining sentences in the story. After the students finish the story, present the following questions.)

8. Everybody, what did Sam read? (Signal.) *The paper.*

   And what did the paper tell Sam? (Signal.) *How to make the car.*

9. Everybody, what kind of kit will Sam get next? (Signal.) *A kite kit.*

Reassessing the Students

After you have completed the remedial exercises, reassess each student individually. To administer the reassessment, you will need the student's Assessment Book, a blank copy of the Assessment Book, and a red pencil. Assess the student in a corner of the classroom, so that the other students will not overhear the assessment. Give the student the blank copy of the Assessment Book. Say, "Look at page 6. You're going to take this assessment again. Read each item aloud and tell me the answer."

You should use the student's own Assessment Book to grade the reassessment. Use the red pencil to mark each correct answer with a *C* and each incorrect answer with an *X*. Then count one point for each correct answer and write the new score at the top of the page.

After grading the reassessment, revise the student's Individual Skills Profile Chart by drawing an *X* over any items the student missed on the reassessment. Then write the new score in the *final score* box.

Recording Group Results

Look at the Individual Checkout Chart and count up the number of stars each student earned on the checkouts for lessons 65 to 80. Then enter the total in the *left* side of the appropriate boxes on the Group Point Chart. Enter the students' final assessment scores in the *right* side of each box.

Assessed Skills

The Lesson 80 curriculum-based assessment measures student mastery of the following skills:

- answering literal questions about a text (items 5 and 8)
- following written directions (items 1–3)
- predicting narrative outcomes (item 7)
- inferring story details and events (item 6)
- interpreting a character's motives (item 4)

Lesson 100

Administering the Assessment

The Lesson 100 curriculum-based assessment should be administered after the students complete all work on lesson 100 and before they begin work on lesson 101. To administer the assessment, you will need a Assessment Book and a pencil for each student. Use the following script:

1. (Direct the students to clear their desks and make sure that each student has a pencil.)

2. Now you're going to take another assessment in your Assessment Book. Do not open the book until I tell you.

3. (Pass out the Assessment Books.)

4. Everybody, open your Assessment Book to page 8. ✔

5. You're going to take the assessment on your own. Let's go over the things you're going to do.

6. Look at items 1 through 3. ✔
   • For items 1 through 3, you will do what the instructions tell you to do.

7. Now look at items 4 and 5. ✔
   • For items 4 and 5, you will read the rule in the box. Then you will do what the instructions tell you to do.

8. Now look at items 6 through 10. ✔
   • For items 6 through 10, you will read the story and then circle the correct answers.

9. Begin the assessment now. There is no time limit. When you are finished, close your Assessment Book and look up at me.

Grading the Assessment

Use the answer key in the next column to grade each assessment. If an answer is correct, mark it with a *C.* If an answer is wrong, mark it with an *X.* Count up the number of *correct* answers and enter the score at the top of the assessment.

Answer Key

Sid was reading notes that his boss had left for him. But Sid was not reading the notes the right way. One note told him to send a cone to a tree farm. But Sid sent a con to a tree farm. Another note told Sid to tape the oak tree near the door. But Sid tapped that tree. The last note told Sid to tape a cup near the door.

6. Who left the notes for Sid?
   • **His boss**   • A con   • A cop

7. One note told Sid to send a _____ to a tree farm.
   • con   • tree   • **cone**

8. But what did Sid send to a tree farm?
   • **A con**   • A tree   • A cone

9. Why didn't Sid do what the notes told him to do?
   • He did not want to work for his boss.
   • He did not want to tape trees.
   • He did not read the notes the right way.

10. The last note told Sid to tape a cup near the door. What will Sid do?
    • Tap a cup near the door
    • Tape a cup near the door
    • Drink a cup near the door

Recording Individual Results

After you have graded the assessments, enter the assessment results on each student's Individual Skills Profile Chart. Circle any items that the student missed, and then count up the number of items that you did *not* circle and enter the total in the *total* box. If the student scored 0 to 7 points, make an *R* in the *reassessment* box. If the student scored 8 to 10 points, write the score in the *final score* box.

Remedial Exercises

Students who scored 0 to 7 points on the assessment should be given remedial help. After the regular reading period is over, assemble these students and present the following exercises. The students will need their marked Assessment Books, but not pencils.

EXERCISE 1   Following Directions

1. Everybody, open your Assessment Book to page 8. ✔

2. Touch the box above item 1. ✔
- (Call on a student.) Read the sentence in the box. *The boy sat under the tree.*

3. Everybody, where did the boy sit? (Signal.) *Under the tree.*

4. Now touch item 1. ✔
- (Call on a student.) Read item 1. *Make a box around the words that tell where the boy sat.*

5. Everybody, where did the boy sit? (Signal.) *Under the tree.*
- So what words will you make a box around? (Signal.) *Under the tree.*

6. Everybody, touch the box above item 2. ✔
- (Call on a student.) Read the sentence in the box. *The goat was on the road.*

7. Everybody, who was on the road? (Signal.) *The goat.*

8. Now touch item 2. ✔
- (Call on a student.) Read item 2. *Circle the words that tell who was on the road.*

9. Everybody, what words will you circle. (Signal.) *The goat.*

10. Everybody, touch the box above item 3. ✔
- (Call on a student.) Read the sentence in the box. *A big dog ran fast.*

11. Everybody, touch item 3. ✔
- (Call on a student.) Read item 3. *Make a line over the word ran.*

12. Everybody, what word will you make a line over? (Signal.) *Ran.*

EXERCISE 2　Using rules

1. Everybody, touch the box above item 4. ✔
- (Call on a student.) Read the rule in the box. *All the spotted pigs are sad.*
- Everybody, say that rule. (Signal.) *All the spotted pigs are sad.*

2. Everybody, look at the pictures of pigs. You know that some of the pigs are sad. Which pigs are sad? (Signal.) *The spotted pigs.*
- Everybody, touch a pig that you know is sad. ✔

3. Everybody, touch item 4. ✔
- (Call on a student.) Read item 4. *Circle the pigs that are sad.*
- Everybody, what are you going to do? (Signal.) *Circle the pigs that are sad.*

4. Everybody, touch the box above item 5. ✔
- (Call on a student.) Read the rule in the box. *All the small horses are tired.*

5. Everybody, look at the pictures of horses. Touch a horse that you know is tired. ✔

EXERCISE 3　Story Reading

1. Everybody, touch the story on page 9. ✔
- Get ready to read the story.

2. (Call on individual students to read several sentences each. Correct all decoding errors. When the students finish, present the following questions.)

3. Everybody, what did the boss leave for Sid? (Signal.) *Notes.*

4. Everybody, one note told Sid to send something to a tree farm. What was he supposed to send? (Signal.) *A cone.*
- But what did Sid send instead? (Signal.) A con.

5. Everybody, did Sid know how to read the right way? (Signal.) No.
- So did Sid do what the notes told him to do? (Signal.) No.

6. Everybody, what did the last note tell Sid to do? (Signal.) Tape a cup near the door.
- But what will Sid do instead? (Signal.) Tap a cup near the door.

Reassessing the Students

After you have completed the remedial exercises, reassess each student individually. To administer the reassessment, you will need the student's Assessment Book, a blank copy of the Assessment Book, and a red pencil. Assess the student in a corner of the classroom, so that the other students will not overhear the assessment. Give the student the blank copy of the Assessment Book. Say, "Look at page 8. You're going to take this assessment again. Read each item aloud and tell me the answer."

You should use the student's own Assessment Book to grade the reassessment. Use the red pencil to mark each correct answer with a *C* and each incorrect answer with an *X*. Then count one point for each correct answer and write the new score at the top of the page.

After grading the reassessment, revise the student's Individual Skills Profile Chart by drawing an *X* over any items the student missed on the reassessment. Then write the new score in the *final score* box.

Recording Group Results

Look at the Individual Checkout Chart and count up the number of stars each student earned on the checkouts for lessons 85 to 100. Then enter the total in the *left* side of the appropriate boxes on the Group Point Chart. Enter the students' final assessment scores in the *right* side of each box.

Assessed Skills

The Lesson 100 curriculum-based assessment measures student mastery of the following skills:

- answering literal questions about a text (items 6–8)
- identifying literal cause and effect (item 9)
- following written directions (items 1–3)
- predicting narrative outcomes (item 10)
- using rules to classify objects (items 4–5)

Lesson 120

Administering the Assessment

The Lesson 120 curriculum-based assessment should be administered after the students complete all work on lesson 120 and before they begin work on lesson 121. To administer the assessment, you will need a Assessment Book and a pencil for each student. Use the following script:

1. (Direct the students to clear their desks and make sure that each student has a pencil.)
    *   Now you're going to take another assessment in your Assessment Book. Do not open the book until I tell you. (Pass out the Assessment Books.)
    *   Everybody, open your Assessment Book to page 10. ✔
    *   You're going to take the assessment on your own. Let's go over the things you're going to do.

2. Look at items 1 and 2. ✔
    *   For items 1 and 2, you will circle the correct answers.

3. Now look at items 3 and 4. ✔
    *   For items 3 and 4, you will do what the instructions tell you to do.

4. Now look at item 5. ✔
    *   For item 5, you will read the rule in the box. Then you will do what the instructions tell you to do.

5. Now look at items 6 through 10. ✔
    *   For items 6 through 10, you will read the story and then circle the correct answers.

6. Begin the assessment now. There is no time limit. When you are finished, close your Assessment Book and look up at me.

Grading the Assessment

Use the answer key in the next column to grade each assessment. If an answer is correct, mark it with a *C.* If an answer is wrong, mark it with an *X.* Count up the number of *correct* answers and enter the score at the top of the assessment.

Answer Key

Lesson 120   Score: **10** possible

1. What did Boo want to get from a monster?
    *   A big frog   *   A mean ghost   *   [A gold rod]

2. What city did Carla and Ott go to?
    *   Nome   *   Ron   *   [Rome]

    [The horses] looked happy.

3. Circle the words that tell who looked happy.

    The man tossed the ball.

4. Make a line under the words that tell what the man tossed.

    If a box has spots, it is made of wood.

5. Circle the boxes that are made of wood.

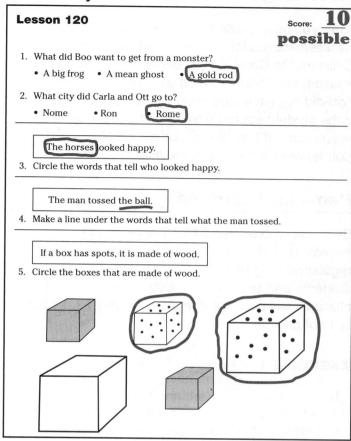

Ott was going to school. He was trying to be a genie, but he did not know many genie tricks.

Genies live in bottles. When somebody rubs the bottle, the genie comes out in a puff of smoke. Then the genie says, "Yes, master, what can I do for you?"

The master tells what he wants, and the genie gets him what he wants. If the master wants an elephant, the genie makes an elephant appear. If the master wants a bag of gold, the genie makes a bag of gold appear.

6. Why was Ott going to school?
    *   He wanted a bag of gold.
    *   (He was trying to be a genie.)
    *   He found a bottle.

7. What do genies live in?
    *   Bags of gold   *   [Bottles]   *   Houses

8. What will a genie do if the master wants a book?
    *   (Make the book appear)
    *   Get the book at a shop
    *   Read the book

9. What happens when the master rubs the bottle?
    *   (The genie comes out of the bottle.)
    *   The genie goes into the bottle.
    *   The bottle turns into a puff of smoke.

10. Who tells what he wants?
    *   The genie   *   Ott   *   [The master]

Recording Individual Results

After you have graded the assessments, enter the assessment results on each student's Individual Skills Profile Chart. Circle any items that the student missed, and then count up the number of items that you did *not* circle and enter the total in the *total* box. If the student scored 0 to 7 points, make an *R* in the *reassessment* box. If the student scored 8 to 10 points, write the score in the *final score* box.

Remedial Exercises

Students who scored 0 to 7 points on the assessment should be given remedial help. After the regular reading period is over, assemble these students and present the following exercises. The students will need their marked Assessment Books, but not pencils.

EXERCISE 1   Recalling Details and Events

1. You read a story about a ghost. Everybody, what was the ghost's name? (Signal.) *Boo.*
- Everybody, who had the gold rod that Boo wanted? (Signal.) *A monster.*

2. Everybody, what kind of place is Rome? (Signal.) *A city.*
- You are reading about a genie who went to Rome.
- Everybody, what is the genie's name? (Signal.) *Ott.*

EXERCISE 2   Following Directions

1. Everybody, open your Assessment Book to page 10. ✔

2. Touch the box above item 3. ✔
- (Call on a student.) Read the sentence in the box. *The horses looked happy.*
- Everybody, how did the horses look? (Signal.) *Happy.*
- Touch the word that tells how the horses looked. ✔

3. Everybody, touch the box above item 4. ✔
- (Call on a student.) Read the sentence in the box. *The man tossed the ball.*
- Everybody, who tossed the ball? (Signal.) *The man.*

EXERCISE 3   Using rules

1. Here's a rule: **If a box is gray, it is made of plastic.** Everybody, say that rule. (Signal.) *If a box is gray, it is made of plastic.*

2. Everybody, look at the pictures under item 5. You know that some of the boxes are made of plastic. Which boxes are made of plastic? (Signal.) *The gray boxes.*
- Everybody, touch a box that you know is made of plastic. ✔

EXERCISE 4   Story Reading

1. Everybody, touch the story on page 11. ✔
- Get ready to read the story.

2. (Call on individual students to read several sentences each. Correct all decoding errors. When the students finish, present the following questions.)

3. Everybody, who was going to school? (Signal.) *Ott.*
- And what was Ott learning at school? (Idea: *How to be a genie.*)

4. What kind of people live in bottles. (Signal.) *Genies.*
- And how do you a get a genie out of the bottle? (Idea: *By rubbing the bottle.*)

5. Who tells what he wants? (Signal.) *The master.*
- Who does things for the master? (Signal.) *The genie.*

6. What will the genie do if the master wants an elephant? Idea: *Make an elephant appear.*
- And what will the genie do if the master wants a bag of gold? Idea: *Make a bag of gold appear.*

Reassessing the Students

After you have completed the remedial exercises, reassess each student individually. To administer the reassessment, you will need the student's Assessment Book, a blank copy of the Assessment Book, and a red pencil. Assess the student in a corner of the classroom, so that the other students will not overhear the assessment. Give the student the blank copy of the Assessment Book. Say, "Look at page 10. You're going to take this assessment again. Read each item aloud and tell me the answer."

You should use the student's own Assessment Book to grade the reassessment. Use the red pencil to mark each correct answer with a *C* and each incorrect answer with an *X*. Then count one point for each correct answer and write the new score at the top of the page.

After grading the reassessment, revise the student's Individual Skills Profile Chart by drawing an *X* over any items the student missed on the reassessment. Then write the new score in the *final score* box.

Recording Group Results

Look at the Individual Checkout Chart and count up the number of stars each student earned on the checkouts for lessons 105 to 120. Then enter the total in the *left* side of the appropriate boxes on the Group Point Chart. Enter the students' final assessment scores in the *right* side of each box.

Assessed Skills

The lesson 120 curriculum-based assessment measures student mastery of the following skills:

- answering literal questions about a text (items 7 and 10)
- identifying literal cause and effect (item 9)
- recalling details and events (items 1–2)
- following written directions (items 3–4)
- predicting narrative outcomes (item 8)
- using rules to classify objects (item 5)
- interpreting a character's motives (item 6)

Lesson 140

Administering the Assessment

The Lesson 140 curriculum-based assessment should be administered after the students complete all work on lesson 140 and before they begin work on lesson 141. To administer the assessment, you will need a Assessment Book and a pencil for each student. Use the following script:

1. (Direct the students to clear their desks and make sure that each student has a pencil.)

2. Now you're going to take another assessment in your Assessment Book. Do not open the book until I tell you.

3. (Pass out the Assessment Books.)

4. Everybody, open your Assessment Book to page 12. ✔

5. You're going to take the assessment on your own. Let's go over the things you're going to do.

6. Look at items 1 through 3. ✔

   • For items 1 through 3, you will circle the correct answers.

7. Now look at items 4 and 5. ✔

   • For items 4 and 5, you will read the rule in the box. Then you will do what the instructions tell you to do.

8. Now look at items 6 through 10. ✔

   • For items 6 through 10, you will read the story and then circle the correct answers.

9. Begin the assessment now. There is no time limit. When you are finished, close your Assessment Book and look up at me.

Grading the Assessment

Use the answer key in the next column to grade each assessment. If an answer is correct, mark it with a C. If an answer is wrong, mark it with an X. Count up the number of *correct* answers and enter the score at the top of the assessment.

Answer Key

Lesson 140   Score: **10** possible

1. What did Carla do to a rock?
   • Turned it into dust
   • Made it hot
   • ~~Turned it into water~~

2. What happened when Kim phoned for a truck?
   • She got a van
   • ~~She got a trunk.~~
   • She got a truck.

3. All blips have red noses.
   Bimbo is a blip.
   So what does Bimbo have?
   • ~~A red nose~~   • A blip   • A bad nose

Hector will sell every bottle that is big and square.

4. Circle the bottles that Hector will sell.

Every fat bird has a nest.

5. Circle the birds that have nests.

There once was a boy who had to watch a flock of sheep. But the boy didn't like his job. One day, he said to himself, "I am tired of watching sheep. I think I'll run into town and play a good joke on the people. I will tell them that a big wolf has come to eat the sheep."

So the boy ran into town and began to shout, "Wolf, wolf. A big wolf is eating the sheep."

The people ran to the flock of sheep. When they got there, the boy started to laugh. "ha, ha," he said. "I played a good joke on you. There is no wolf here."

The boy's father said, "That is not a good joke. Some day a wolf will come and eat the sheep. But nobody will believe you when you yell, 'Wolf, wolf.' "

6. How did the boy feel about his job?
   • He liked it a lot.   • ~~He didn't like it.~~   • He was scared of it.

7. Why did the boy run into town and yell "Wolf, wolf"?
   • ~~He wanted to play a joke.~~
   • A wolf was eating the sheep.
   • He wanted to see his father.

8. Why did the people run to the flock of sheep?
   • They wanted to hear a good joke.
   • ~~They wanted to save the sheep.~~
   • They wanted to eat the sheep.

9. What will happen when a real wolf comes and the boy yells "Wolf, wolf"?
   • ~~No one will believe the boy.~~
   • Everyone will believe the boy.
   • The wolf will not eat the sheep.

10. Who said, "That is not a good joke"?
    • ~~The boy's father~~   • The boy   • The wolf

Recording Individual Results

After you have graded the assessments, enter the assessment results on each student's Individual Skills Profile Chart. Circle any items that the student missed, and then count up the number of items that you did *not* circle and enter the total in the *total* box. If the student scored 0 to 7 points, make an *R* in the *reassessment* box. If the student scored 8 to 10 points, write the score in the *final score* box.

Remedial Exercises

Students who scored 0 to 7 points on the assessment should be given remedial help. After the regular reading period is over, assemble these students and present the following exercises. The students will need their marked Assessment Books, but not pencils.

EXERCISE 1   Recalling Details and Events

1. You read a story about Carla. Everybody, what kind of school did Carla go to? (Signal.) *A genie school.*
- Everybody, what objects could Carla turn into water? (Signal.) *Rocks.*

2. You read a story about someone who could not spell well.
- Everybody, what was that person's name? (Signal.) *Kim.*
- What did Kim get the first time she phoned for a van? (Signal.) *A vane.*
- What did Kim get when she phoned for a rental car? (Signal.) *False teeth.*

EXERCISE 2   Using rules

1. Here's a rule: **All mibs have green feet.** Everybody, say that rule. (Signal.) *All mibs have green feet.*

2. Everybody, Rover is a mib. So what else do you know about Rover? (Signal.) *He has green feet.*

3. Everybody, open your Assessment Book to page 12. ✔

4. Here's a rule: **Maria owns all the round bottles.** Everybody, say that rule. (Signal.) *Maria owns all the round bottles.*

5. Everybody, look at the picture under item 4. You know that Maria owns some of the bottles. Which bottles does Maria own? (Signal.) *The round bottles.*
- Everybody, touch a bottle that you know Maria owns. ✔

6. Here's another rule: **Every skinny bird lays eggs.** Everybody, say that rule. (Signal.)

7. Everybody, look at the pictures under item 5. Point to a bird that you know lays eggs. ✔

EXERCISE 3   Story Reading

1. Everybody, touch the story on page 13. ✔
- Get ready to read the story.

2. (Call on individual students to read several sentences each. Correct all decoding errors. When the students finish, present the following questions.)

3. Everybody, did the boy like his job? (Signal.) *No.*

4. Everybody, what did the boy yell when he ran into town? (Signal.) *Wolf, wolf.*

5. Everybody, when the boy yelled, was he **telling the truth or playing a joke?** (Signal.) *Playing a joke.*

6. What did the people do when the boy yelled **wolf, wolf?** (Idea: Ran to the sheep.)
- Why did the people do that? (Idea: They wanted to save the sheep.)

7. Everybody, did the boy's father think that the boy had made a good joke? (Signal.) *No.*

8. Everybody, will the people believe the boy the next time he yells **wolf, wolf?** (Signal.) *No.*
- Why won't they believe him? (Idea: They'll think he's making a joke.)

Reassessing the Students

After you have completed the remedial exercises, reassess each student individually. To administer the reassessment, you will need the student's Assessment Book, a blank copy of the Assessment Book, and a red pencil. Assess the student in a corner of the classroom, so that the other students will not overhear the assessment. Give the student the blank copy of the Assessment Book. Say, "Look at page 12. You're going to take this assessment again. Read each item aloud and tell me the answer."

You should use the student's own Assessment Book to grade the reassessment. Use the red pencil to mark each correct answer with a *C* and each incorrect answer with an *X*. Then count one point for each correct answer and write the new score at the top of the page.

After grading the reassessment, revise the student's Individual Skills Profile Chart by drawing an *X* over any items the student missed on the reassessment. Then write the new score in the *final score* box.

Recording Group Results

Look at the Individual Checkout Chart and count up the number of stars each student earned on the checkouts for lessons 125 to 140. Then enter the total in the *left* side of the appropriate boxes on the Group Point Chart. Enter the students' final assessment scores in the *right* side of each box.

Assessed Skills

The Lesson 140 curriculum-based assessment measures student mastery of the following skills:

- answering literal questions about a text (item 10)
- recalling details and events (items 1–2)
- predicting narrative outcomes (item 9)
- inferring causes and effects (item 8)
- using rules to classify objects (items 4–5)
- completing written deductions (item 3)
- interpreting a character's feelings (item 6)
- interpreting a character's motives (item 7)

Lesson 160

Administering the Assessment

The Lesson 160 curriculum-based assessment should be administered after the students complete all work on lesson 160. To administer the assessment, you will need a Assessment Book and a pencil for each student. Use the following script:

1. (Direct the students to clear their desks and make sure that each student has a pencil.)

2. Now you're going to take another assessment in your Assessment Book. Do not open the book until I tell you.

3. (Pass out the Assessment Books.)

4. Everybody, open your Assessment Book to page 14. ✔

5. You're going to take the assessment on your own. Let's go over the things you're going to do.

6. Look at items 1 through 5. ✔

• For items 1 through 5, you will circle the correct answers.

7. Now look at items 6 through 10. ✔

• For items 6 through 10, you will read the story and then circle the correct answers.

8. Begin the assessment now. There is no time limit. When you are finished, close your Assessment Book and look up at me.

Grading the Assessment

Use the answer key in the next column to grade each assessment. If an answer is correct, mark it with a *C*. If an answer is wrong, mark it with an *X*. Count up the number of *correct* answers and enter the score at the top of the assessment.

Answer Key

Lesson 160　　　　　Score: **10** possible

1. What is the rule about dusty paths?
   • Every dusty path leads to the lake.
   • Every dusty path leads to the mountain.
   • Every dusty path leads to a crump.

2. What is the rule about being cold?
   • If you want to be cold, stand on one foot.
   • If you want to be cold, say "side, slide."
   • If you want to be cold, clap your hands.

3. All lerms have green hair
   Oscar is a lerm.
   So what do you know about Oscar?
   • His hair has lerms.
   • He has green hair.
   • His hair is gray.

4. Here's a rule: Every short boy has red hair.
   Which person has red hair?
   • A short girl named Jan
   • A short boy named Sid
   • A tall boy named Tim

5. Here's a rule: Every brown hat is full of dirt.
   Which hat is full of dirt?
   • A hat that is not brown
   • A hat that is red
   • A hat that is brown

Jean met a talking bug. She said to herself, "this is a talking animal. I know the rule about talking animals: All talking animals lie."

The bug said, "I will tell you a good joke."

Jean had an idea about how to trick the talking animal. She said to herself, "If this animal says that a joke will be good, it won't be good. And if he says that a joke will be bad, it won't be bad."

Jean smiled to herself. "I will ask him to tell me a joke that is really bad. But he won't tell me a joke that is really bad. He will tell me a joke that is really good."

6. What is the rule about talking animals?
   • All walking animals lie.
   • All talking animals lie.
   • No talking animals lie.

7. If the bug says that something will be good, that thing will be _____
   • good　　• wet　　• bad

8. If the bug says that something is cold, that thing will be _____.
   • cold　　• dry　　• hot

9. Why will Jean ask the bug to tell a really bad joke?
   • She wants to hear a really bad joke.
   • She wants to hear a really good joke.
   • She wants to hear a really good and bad joke.

10. What will Jean do if she wants something wet?
    • Ask the bug for something wet
    • Ask the bug for something dry
    • Ask the bug for water

Recording Individual Results

After you have graded the assessments, enter the assessment results on each student's Individual Skills Profile Chart. Circle any items that the student missed, and then count up the number of items that you did *not* circle and enter the total in the *total* box. If the student scored 0 to 7 points, make an *R* in the *reassessment* box. If the student scored 8 to 10 points, write the score in the *final score* box.

Remedial Exercises

Students who scored 0 to 7 points on the assessment should be given remedial help. After the regular reading period is over, assemble these students and present the following exercises. The students will need their marked Assessment Books, but not pencils.

EXERCISE 1   Recalling Details and Events

1. You learned a rule about red food. Everybody, say that rule. Get ready. (Signal.) *Red food is good to eat.*

2. You learned a rule about dusty paths. Everybody, say that rule. Get ready. (Signal.) *Every dusty path leads to the lake.*

3. You learned a rule about if you eat three red bananas. Everybody, say that rule. Get ready. (Signal.) *If you eat three red bananas, you get red stripes.*

4. You learned a rule about being cold. Everybody, say that rule. Get ready. (Signal.) *If you want to be cold, say "side slide."*

EXERCISE 2   Using rules

1. Here's a rule: **Every gorp has brown ears.** Everybody, say that rule. (Signal.) *Every gorp has brown ears.*

2. Everybody, Zeno is a gorp. So what else do you know about him? (Signal.) *He has brown ears.*

3. Here is another rule: **Every boy is wearing sneakers.** Everybody, say that rule. (Signal.) *Every boy is wearing sneakers.*

4. Everybody, Tammy is a girl. So do we know if Tammy is wearing sneakers? (Signal.) *No.*
* Everybody, Jim is a boy. So is Jim wearing sneakers? (Signal.) *Yes.*

5. Here is another rule: **Every green car has a flat tire.** Everybody, say that rule. (Signal.) *Every green car has a flat tire.*

6. Everybody, Hector has a green car. So does Hector's car have a flat tire? (Signal.) *Yes.*
* Everybody, Yvonne has a red car. So do you know if Yvonne's car has a flat tire? (Signal.) *No.*

EXERCISE 3   Story Reading

1. Everybody, open your Assessment Book to page 15. ✔
- Get ready to read the story.

2. (Call on individual students to read several sentences each. Correct all decoding errors. When the students finish, present the following questions.)

3. Everybody, is the bug a talking animal? (Signal.) *Yes.*
- And what do all talking animals do? (Signal.) *Lie.*

4. If the bug says that something will be bad, what will that thing be like? (Signal.) *Good.*
- If the bug says that something will be little, what will that thing be like? (Signal.) *Big.*

5. If Jean wants to hear a really bad joke, what will she ask the bug to do? (Idea: *Tell a really good joke.*)

Reassessing the Students

After you have completed the remedial exercises, reassess each student individually. To administer the reassessment, you will need the student's Assessment Book, a blank copy of the Assessment Book, and a red pencil. Assess the student in a corner of the classroom, so that the other students will not overhear the assessment. Give the student the blank copy of the Assessment Book. Say, "Look at page 14. You're going to take this assessment again. Read each item aloud and tell me the answer."

You should use the student's own Assessment Book to grade the reassessment. Use the red pencil to mark each correct answer with a *C* and each incorrect answer with an *X*. Then count one point for each correct answer and write the new score at the top of the page.

After grading the reassessment, revise the student's Individual Skills Profile Chart by drawing an *X* over any items the student missed on the reassessment. Then write the new score in the *final score* box.

Recording Group Results

Look at the Individual Checkout Chart and count up the number of stars each student earned on the checkouts for lessons 145 to 160. Then enter the total in the *left* side of the appropriate boxes on the Group Point Chart. Enter the students' final assessment scores in the *right* side of each box.

Assessed Skills

The Lesson 160 curriculum-based assessment measures student mastery of the following skills:

- answering literal questions about a text (item 6)
- identifying literal cause and effect (item 7)
- applying facts and rules (items 1–2)
- predicting narrative outcomes (item 10)
- inferring story details and events (item 8)
- using rules to classify objects (items 4–5)
- completing written deductions (item 3)
- interpreting a character's motives (item 9)

Appendix

Fluency: Rate/Accuracy Checkouts

Individual Fluency Checkout Chart

Lessons / Names	5	10	15	20	25	30	35	40	45	50	55	60	65	70	75	80
2 stars possible	2	2	2	2	2	2	2	2	2	2	2	2	2	2	2	2

Lessons / Names	85	90	95	100	105	110	115	120	125	130	135	140	145	150	155	160
2 stars possible	2	2	2	2	2	2	2	2	2	2	2	2	2	2	2	2

Fluency: Rate/Accuracy Checkouts

Fluency: Rate/Accuracy Checkout Recording Form

Student performance should be recorded as total time over number of errors. (for example John: 1:42/2)

Lessons	5	10	15	20	25	30	35	40	45	50	55	60	65	70	75	80
Minutes / Errors	2½ / 3	2½ / 3	2½ / 3	2 / 3	2 / 4	2 / 3	2½ / 4	2 / 3	2½ / 4	2 / 3	2 / 3	2½ / 4	2½ / 4	2 / 3	2 / 3	2 / 4
Names																

Fluency: Rate/Accuracy Checkouts

Fluency: Rate/Accuracy Checkout Recording Form

Student performance should be recorded as total time over number of errors. (for example John: 1:42/2)

Lessons	85	90	95	100	105	110	115	120	125	130	135	140	145	150	155	160
Minutes / Errors	2/4	2/4	2/4	2/4	2/4	2/5	2/5	2/5	2/5	2/5	2/5	2/5	2/5	2/5	2/5	2/5
Names																

Interpreting the Assessment Results

The assessment results are recorded on both the Individual Skills Profile Chart and the Group Point Chart. Each chart gives a different interpretation of the results. The Individual Skills Profile Chart shows the specific benchmark skills that the students have mastered; the Group Point Chart shows the group's overall performance.

The Individual Skills Profile Chart

The Individual Skills Profile Chart should be used to assess each student's strengths and weaknesses. Assessment items that the student missed on an initial assessment will be circled; items missed on a reassessment will be crossed out. On the sample chart, the student took a reassessment on Lesson 100. Note that some items have been both circled and crossed out on Lesson 100.

If a chart has more than 13 circled or crossed out items, the student may still be weak in certain areas. Look for two general patterns of weakness. In the first pattern, a student will consistently fail items that measure a particular skill. On the sample chart below, for example, the student consistently failed items that measured the skill, "reading irregularly spelled words." Students who fall into this pattern may require further teaching of particular skills.

In the second pattern, a student will do poorly on one assessment but fairly well on the other assessments. On the sample chart below, for example, the student did poorly on the assessment for Lesson 100. Usually, students who fall into this pattern were absent on the days preceding the assessment. These students may profit from a review of the lessons they missed.

Individual Skills Profile Chart Name: **Sample**
Curriculum-Based Assessments Lessons 20-160

Skills / Assessments	20	40	60	80	100	120	140	160
writing the names of pictured objects	1 2							
answering literal questions about a text	3 4 5 ⑥	3 6	4 8	5 8	6 7 ⑧	7 10	10	6
identifying literal cause and effect		4			9	9		7
recalling details and events						1 2	1 2	
following written directions		1 2	1 2 3	1 2 3	1 2 3	3 4		
applying rules								1 2
predicting narrative outcomes		⑤	⑤	⑦	⑩	⑧	⑨	⑩
inferring causes and effects				6			8	
inferring story details and events					6			⑧
using rules to classify objects					4 ⊗	5	4 5	4 5
completing written deductions							3	3
interpreting a character's feelings				7			⑥	
interpreting a character's motives					4	6	7	9
Total	**5**	**5**	**7**	**7**	**7**	**9**	**8**	**9**
Reassessment					**R**			
FINAL SCORE	**5**	**5**	**7**	**7**	**9**	**9**	**8**	**9**

(Left vertical label: Comprehension and Literary Skills)

Individual Skills Profile Chart

Name: _____

Curriculum-Based Assessments Lessons 20-160

Skills — Assessments	20	40	60	80	100	120	140	160
writing the names of pictured objects	1 2							
answering literal questions about a text	3 4 5 6	3 6	4 8	5 8	6 7 8	7 10	10	6
identifying literal cause and effect		4			9	9		7
recalling details and events						1 2	1 2	
following written directions		1 2	1 2 3	1 2 3	1 2 3	3 4		
applying rules								1 2
predicting narrative outcomes		5	5	7	10	8	9	10
inferring causes and effects			6				8	
inferring story details and events				6				8
using rules to classify objects					4 5	5	4 5	4 5
completing written deductions							3	3
interpreting a character's feelings			7				6	
interpreting a character's motives				4		6	7	9
Total								
Reassessment								
FINAL SCORE								

(Left vertical label: **Comprehension and Literary Skills**)

The Group Point Chart

The Group Point Chart should be used to assess the group's overall performance. Before interpreting the Group Point Chart, it is necessary to complete the final two columns of the chart for each student.

1. Add the scores in the left side of each box and enter the total in the column labeled "checkouts".
2. Add the scores in the right side of each box and enter the total in the column labeled "CBA".

The completed sample chart shows each student's final totals for the fluency checkouts and the curriculum-based assessments.

Because the fluency checkouts and the curriculum-based assessments measure different types of skills, you should evaluate each total separately.

The fluency checkouts measure decoding fluency and accuracy. The students can earn a maximum of 64 points on the checkouts. Students who score 32 to 64 points on the fluency checkouts have probably mastered the decoding skills taught in the program.

The curriculum-based assessments measure comprehension skills and literary skills. The students can earn a maximum of 68 points on the 8 assessments. Students who score 55 to 68 points on the curriculum-based assessments have probably mastered the comprehension and literary skills taught in the program.

Group Point Chart: Checkouts and Curriculum-Based Assessments

Lessons	20	40	60	80	100	120	140	160	check-outs	CBA
Highest possible number of stars / Highest possible assessment score	8 / 6	8 / 6	8 / 8	8 / 8	8 / 10	8 / 10	8 / 10	8 / 10	64	68
Lupe Baco	6 / 5	6 / 5	7 / 7	7 / 8	8 / 8	6 / 8	7 / 9	8 / 8	55	58
Tatsu Boki	8 / 5	8 / 5	6 / 8	7 / 7	6 / 19	6 / 9	7 / 8	8 / 9	56	61
Don Clark	7 / 5	6 / 5	6 / 7	7 / 7	8 / 9	5 / 9	6 / 8	7 / 9	32	59

Group Point Chart: Checkouts and Curriculum-Based Assessments

Lessons	20	40	60	80	100	120	140	160	check-outs	CBA
Highest possible number of stars / Highest possible assessment score	8 / 6	8 / 6	8 / 8	8 / 8	8 / 10	8 / 10	8 / 10	8 / 10	64	68

Additional Resources

Reading Mastery, Grade 1 — Individual Fluency: Rate/Accuracy Checkout Recording Form

Names	Check-out	1	2	3	4	5	6	7	8	9	10	11	12	13	14	15	16
	After Lesson	5	10	15	20	25	30	35	40	45	50	55	60	65	70	75	80
	Time/ #errors	2:30/3	2:00/3	2:00/3	2:00/3	2:00/43	3:00/3	3:00/4	3:00/3	2:30/43	3:00/3	3:30/3	2:34/3	2:30/4	2:30/3	2:30/3	2:30/4
	Average	45 wpm	40 wpm	40 wpm	43 wpm	52 wpm	50 wpm	47 wpm	52 wpm	51 wpm	53 wpm	52 wpm	58 wpm	52 wpm	55 wpm	60 wpm	60 wpm
Retest																	
Retest																	
Retest																	
Retest																	
Retest																	
Retest																	
Retest																	
Retest																	
Retest																	
Retest																	
Retest																	
Retest																	
Retest																	
Retest																	

- Checkouts are administered individually.
- Students read a selection (from today's story) within a specified time and error limit.
- Time and errors vary from checkout to checkout, but are always stated in the Teacher Presentation Book.
- Student performance should be recorded as total time over number of errors.
- If teachers want to keep a "star chart" as the teacher materials suggest, then a chart is provided in this handbook on page 79.

Reading Mastery Grade 1

Reading Mastery, Grade 1 Individual Fluency: Rate/Accuracy Checkout Recording Form

Names	Check-out	17	18	19	20	21	22	23	24	25	26	27	28	29	30	31	32
	After Lesson	85	90	95	100	105	110	115	120	125	130	135	140	145	150	155	160
	Time/ #errors	2:00/4	2:00/4	2:00/4	2:00/4	2:00/4	2:00/5	2:00/5	2:00/5	2:00/5	2:00/5	2:00/5	2:00/5	2:00/5	2:00/5	2:00/5	2:00/5
	Average	60 wpm	60 wpm	60 wpm	60 wpm	60 wpm	70 wpm	70 wpm	75 wpm	75 wpm	74 wpm	75 wpm	80 wpm	80 wpm	90 wpm	90 wpm	92 wpm
Retest																	
Retest																	
Retest																	
Retest																	
Retest																	
Retest																	
Retest																	
Retest																	
Retest																	
Retest																	

- Checkouts are administered individually.
- Students read a selection (from today's story) within a specified time and error limit.
- Time and errors vary from checkout to checkout, but are always stated in the Teacher Presentation Book.
- Student performance should be recorded as total time over number of errors.
- If teachers want to keep a "star chart" as the teacher materials suggest, then a chart is provided in this handbook on page 79.

The following charts can be used to coordinate instruction for students requiring accelerated movement through the program.

Reading Mastery Accelerated Instruction Schedule

Grade K Schedule

Teach Lesson	Skip Lessons	Teach Lesson	Skip Lessons	Teach Lesson	Skip Lessons	Teach Lesson	Skip Lessons
	1–11		49		83		119
12		50–51		84		120	
	13		52–53		85		121
14		54		86		122	
	15		55		87–89		123–124
16		56		90–91		125–126	
	17–18		57		92		127
19		58		93–95		128	
	20–21		59		95		129
22–23		60–62		96		130	
	24		63		97		131
25–27		64		98		132	
	28		65		99		133–134
29		66–67		100		135	
	30		68		101		136
31		69		102		137–138	
	32		70		103		139
33		71		104–106		140	
	34		72		107		141
35–36		73		108		142	
	37		74		109		143–144
38–39		75–76		110		145–147	
	40		77		111		148–149
41–42		78		112		150	
	43		79		113–114		151
44–45		80		115–116		152	
	46–47		81		117		153–154
48		82		118		155–158	

Grade 1 Schedule

Teach Lesson	Skip Lessons	Teach Lesson	Skip Lessons	Teach Lesson	Skip Lessons	Teach Lesson	Skip Lessons
	1–10		39		59–75		127–132
11-12		40–46		76–94		133–137	
	13–22		47		95–96		138–145
23		48–49		97		146–160	
	24–32		50		98–102		
33–38		51–58		103–126			